W9-AGT-053

LEONTYNE PRICE

VOICE OF A CENTURY

by CAROLE BOSTON WEATHERFORD
illustrated by RAUL COLÓN

ALFRED A. KNOPF
NEW YORK

He's got the whole world in His hands.
—from the spiritual often sung
by Leontyne Price & Marian Anderson

1927. Laurel, Mississippi.

The line between black and white
was as wide as the Mississippi River was long.
All a black girl from the Cotton Belt could expect
was a heap of hard work—as a maid, mill worker, or sharecropper.
Her song, most surely the blues.

Yes, the Mississippi Delta cradled misery,
but from day one, Mary Violet Leontyne Price
heard a different refrain—her mama, Katie, singing hymns;
her daddy, James, playing tuba for the church band;
the flock, greeting praise songs with *hallelujahs*.

Leontyne had plenty to be thankful for.
A mama and daddy who made sure
Leontyne had two pairs of shoes and knew
she was as good as anyone—black or white.
Their song of encouragement
rose above the color line.

Wasn't long before Leontyne was finding her voice.
Singing along to her daddy James's records and listening
to the Metropolitan Opera's Saturday-afternoon radio broadcasts.
She soaked up the sopranos, if not the foreign words.
Art songs and arias, shaping a brown girl's dreams.

Soon, Leontyne was *plink-plink*ing a toy piano
until she caught the performing bug for good.
Her parents sold their phonograph to pay for a real piano—and for lessons.
At her first recital, her feet didn't even reach the pedals.
But the songs came through her fingertips.

Then little Leontyne saw Marian Anderson, the opera singer
from Philadelphia who was already studying in Europe
when Leontyne breathed her first solo.

Marian glided onstage in a whoosh of satin.
Her song, like a torch, sparked a light in Leontyne.

That Easter Sunday in 1939, when Marian sang at the Lincoln Memorial
after being barred from a whites-only concert hall,
Leontyne was in the church choir, praising God with her gift.
A song of promise welled up in Leontyne, as it had in young Marian.

With her suitcase, she rode a bus to college in Ohio,
aiming to be a teacher, the concert stage out of reach for a black singer then.

Until the college president heard her solo and convinced her
to study voice instead. Leontyne changed course.
Led by song, she cracked the door that Marian had opened years earlier.

And before long, Leontyne went to Juilliard. There, she found
her teacher, Florence Page Kimball, and her calling.

But the door to grand opera would have to wait.
First, Leontyne starred on Broadway in *Porgy and Bess*.
On a world tour, her song rose to the rafters.

When the curtain did rise on Leontyne's opera career, she took

bows as Wild West saloon owner Minnie,

as Cio-Cio-San in *Madama Butterfly*,

and as Cleopatra, queen of the Nile.

She became the first black singer to star at La Scala, Italy's famed opera palace. Her song scaled the six tiered balconies and brushed the gilded ceiling.

Yet certain doors her golden songs could not open.
In America, some hotels, restaurants, and stages were still whites-only.

But television brought Leontyne into living rooms.
Viewers saw that skin color didn't matter; voice did.
And her song was as regal as it was rich and rare.

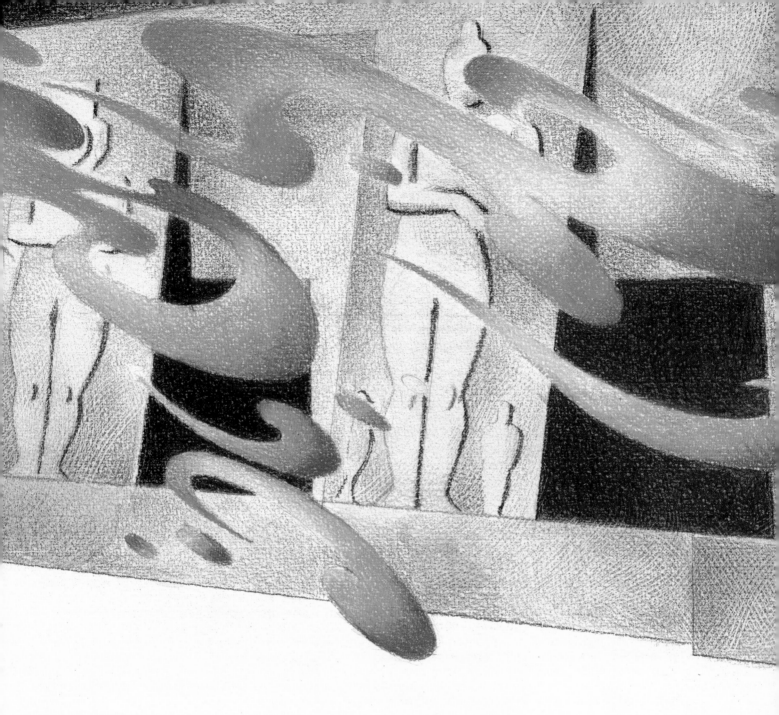

Leontyne was never more majestic than as Aida,
playing the part she was born to sing. As the Ethiopian princess,
with her skin as her costume, she expressed her whole self.
Standing on Marian's shoulders, Leontyne gave the crowd goose bumps.
The song of her soul soared on the breath of her ancestors.

When Leontyne performed at the Metropolitan Opera House in 1955,
she blew open the door that Marian left ajar. Six years later,
Leontyne landed her first lead role with the Met. In *Il Trovatore*,
as a noble lady in a tragic love story, she got a forty-two-minute
standing ovation. The song of roaring applause shook the walls.

Roses at her feet and tears in her eyes, Leontyne bowed.
She glimpsed the spotlight casting a shadow. She knew
that shadow was not just hers, but her parents', teachers',
and Marian's. Back in Laurel, Mississippi,
songs of pride filled many a heart.
The folks there were bowing, too.

Yes, the world-famous Miss Price could be all mink and pearls when she wanted to, rolling her r's like an Italian *contessa*, wearing Viennese hats and silk dresses from Rome.

But offstage, she was just Leontyne, twisting all night long. Her song sure wasn't the blues.

AUTHOR'S NOTE

Born in Laurel, Mississippi, in 1927, Mary Violet Leontyne Price inherited the legacy of Marian Anderson, the first black singer to perform at the Metropolitan Opera House. Anderson gave a historic concert at the Lincoln Memorial after a Washington, D.C., concert hall barred her because it had a white-artists-only policy. A pioneer in her own right, Price was the first black opera singer to perform on television in the United States, and in leading roles at the Met and Italy's famed La Scala opera house.

The daughter of a sawmill worker and a midwife who sang in the church choir, Leontyne showed musical talent at an early age. "Her voice was given to her by God," her mother claimed. After seeing Marian Anderson in concert, young Price envisioned a future onstage. But racism made it unlikely that a black girl from Mississippi would have a career as an opera singer.

Price majored in music education at Wilberforce College, in Ohio, planning to become a teacher and help pay her brother's way through school. Her voice led her in a different direction, though—to change her major to voice, to study at the Juilliard School of Music, and to pursue an opera career after seeing the opera *Turandot.*

Having achieved stardom in the Broadway revival of *Porgy and Bess,* Price got her turn at grand opera after another singer fell ill. A lyric soprano, she dazzled in operas by Puccini, Mozart, and Verdi. The title role in Verdi's *Aida*—as an Ethiopian princess—made Price an international star.

Despite her great fame, Price still encountered racism in the United States. To her credit, her wondrous voice overcame the obstacles. With more than a dozen Grammy Awards, she retired from opera in 1985 with a performance of *Aida,* but graced the concert stage for several more years.

President Lyndon Johnson lauded Price's artistry when he awarded her the Presidential Medal of Freedom. "A voice of stirring power and rare beauty," he proclaimed. "Her singing has brought delight to her land."

The path that Anderson braved, Price paved, making way for African American divas like Jessye Norman, Grace Bumbry, Kathleen Battle, and Denyce Graves.

THIS IS A BORZOI BOOK PUBLISHED BY ALFRED A. KNOPF

Text copyright © 2014 by Carole Boston Weatherford
Jacket art and interior illustrations copyright © 2014 by Raul Colón

All rights reserved. Published in the United States by Alfred A. Knopf, an imprint of Random House Children's Books, a division of Random House LLC, a Penguin Random House Company, New York.

Knopf, Borzoi Books, and the colophon are registered trademarks of Random House LLC.

Visit us on the Web! randomhousekids.com

Educators and librarians, for a variety of teaching tools, visit us at RHTeachersLibrarians.com

Library of Congress Cataloging-in-Publication Data is available upon request.

ISBN 978-0-375-85606-8 (trade) — ISBN 978-0-375-95606-5 (lib. bdg.) — ISBN 978-0-385-39246-4 (ebook)

The text of this book is set in 18-point Deligne.
The illustrations were created in watercolors, Prismacolor pencils, and lithograph crayons on Arches watercolor paper.

MANUFACTURED IN CHINA

December 2014

10 9 8 7 6 5 4 3 2 1

First Edition